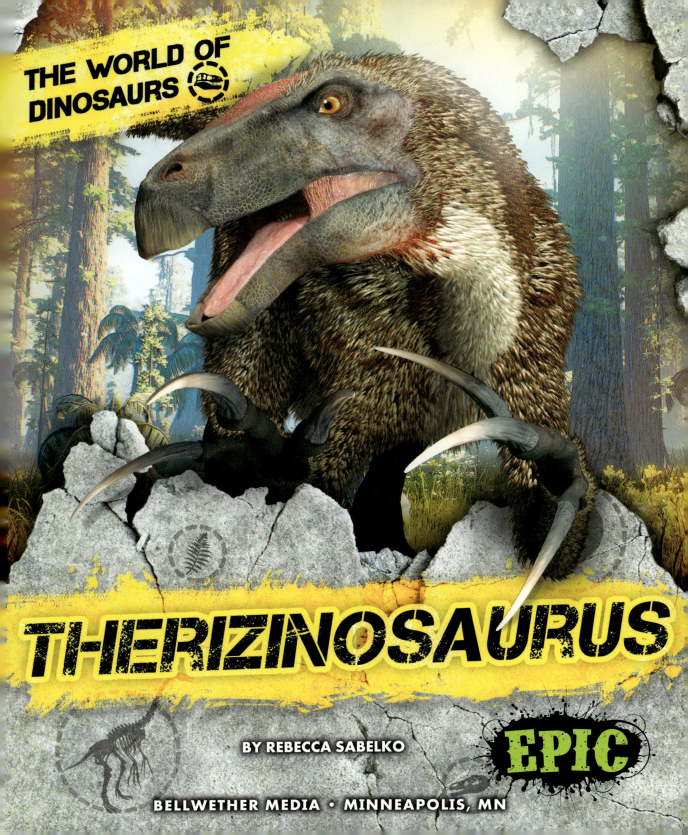

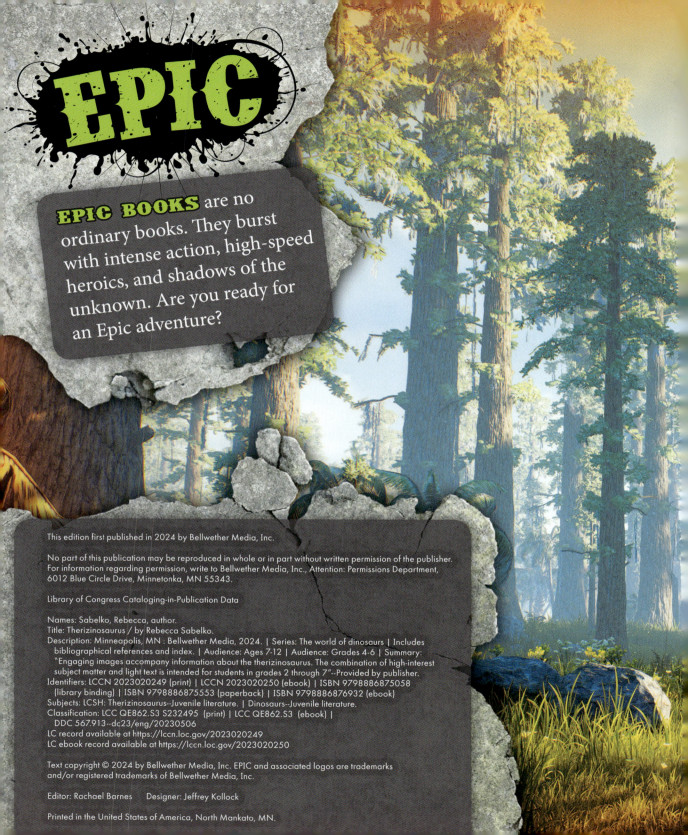

# EPIC

**EPIC BOOKS** are no ordinary books. They burst with intense action, high-speed heroics, and shadows of the unknown. Are you ready for an Epic adventure?

This edition first published in 2024 by Bellwether Media, Inc.

No part of this publication may be reproduced in whole or in part without written permission of the publisher. For information regarding permission, write to Bellwether Media, Inc., Attention: Permissions Department, 6012 Blue Circle Drive, Minnetonka, MN 55343.

Library of Congress Cataloging-in-Publication Data

Names: Sabelko, Rebecca, author.
Title: Therizinosaurus / by Rebecca Sabelko.
Description: Minneapolis, MN : Bellwether Media, 2024. | Series: The world of dinosaurs | Includes bibliographical references and index. | Audience: Ages 7-12 | Audience: Grades 4-6 | Summary: "Engaging images accompany information about the therizinosaurus. The combination of high-interest subject matter and light text is intended for students in grades 2 through 7"--Provided by publisher.
Identifiers: LCCN 2023020249 (print) | LCCN 2023020250 (ebook) | ISBN 9798886875058 (library binding) | ISBN 9798886875553 (paperback) | ISBN 9798886876932 (ebook)
Subjects: LCSH: Therizinosaurus--Juvenile literature. | Dinosaurs--Juvenile literature.
Classification: LCC QE862.S3 S232495 (print) | LCC QE862.S3 (ebook) | DDC 567.913--dc23/eng/20230506
LC record available at https://lccn.loc.gov/2023020249
LC ebook record available at https://lccn.loc.gov/2023020250

Text copyright © 2024 by Bellwether Media, Inc. EPIC and associated logos are trademarks and/or registered trademarks of Bellwether Media, Inc.

Editor: Rachael Barnes    Designer: Jeffrey Kollock

Printed in the United States of America, North Mankato, MN.

# TABLE OF CONTENTS

| | |
|---|---|
| THE WORLD OF THE THERIZINOSAURUS | 4 |
| WHAT WAS THE THERIZINOSAURUS? | 6 |
| DIET AND DEFENSES | 10 |
| FOSSILS AND EXTINCTION | 16 |
| GET TO KNOW THE THERIZINOSAURUS | 20 |
| GLOSSARY | 22 |
| TO LEARN MORE | 23 |
| INDEX | 24 |

# THE WORLD OF THE THERIZINOSAURUS

claws

The therizinosaurus was a dinosaur with 3-foot-long (1-meter-long) claws! Its claws were the longest of any animal to ever live.

## ⚠️ MAP OF THE WORLD

**Late Cretaceous period**

## ⚠️ PRONUNCIATION

**THER-ih-zine-oh-SORE-us**

This dinosaur lived during the Late **Cretaceous period**. This was during the **Mesozoic era**.

5

# WHAT WAS THE THERIZINOSAURUS?

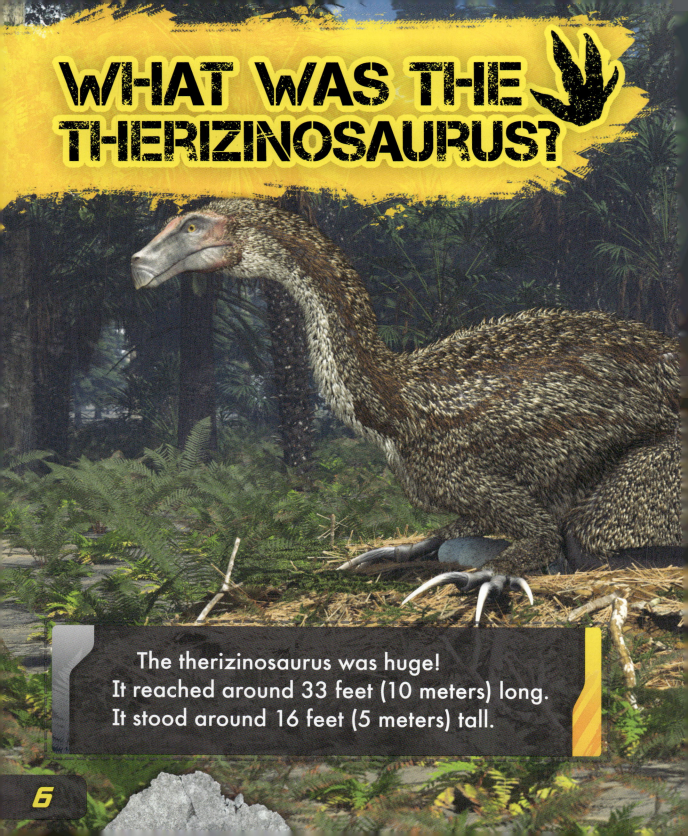

The therizinosaurus was huge! It reached around 33 feet (10 meters) long. It stood around 16 feet (5 meters) tall.

This dinosaur weighed over 11,000 pounds (4,990 kilograms).

SIZE CHART

25 feet (7.6 meters)
15 feet (4.6 meters)
5 feet (1.5 meters)

The therizinosaurus had a small head and long neck. Each arm stretched up to 8 feet (2.4 meters) long.

The dinosaur had wide hips. Its belly was large.

## ⚠️ NAME GAME

The word *therizinosaurus* means "scythe lizard." A scythe is a tool that has a hooked blade.

# DIET AND DEFENSES

The therizinosaurus was a **theropod**. Most theropods were meat eaters.

The therizinosaurus may have eaten small animals. But many scientists believe this dinosaur **evolved** to eat plants. It mostly ate leaves.

## THERIZINOSAURUS DIET

flowering plants

tree leaves

ferns

11

It likely reached for leaves in trees. Its curved claws hooked and pulled branches to its mouth.

The dinosaur plucked leaves with its beak. Its large belly **digested** plants well.

beak

13

The therizinosaurus was hunted by a few large **predators**. It was too slow to run from them.

tarbosaurus

## THE ENEMY

The tarbosaurus hunted the therizinosaurus. This predator had a huge head. Sharp teeth lined its powerful jaws.

The dinosaur may have used its sharp claws to fight enemies. But scientists think its claws were likely too weak.

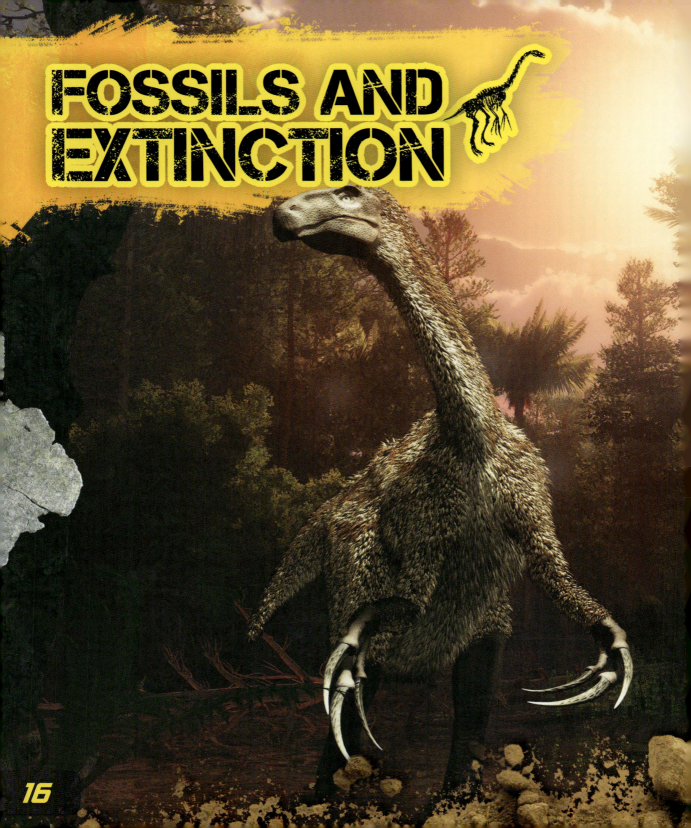

# FOSSILS AND EXTINCTION

16

A huge **asteroid** crashed into Earth around 66 million years ago. The therizinosaurus's **habitat** was destroyed. The dinosaur could not survive.

Most dinosaurs and many other animals went **extinct**.

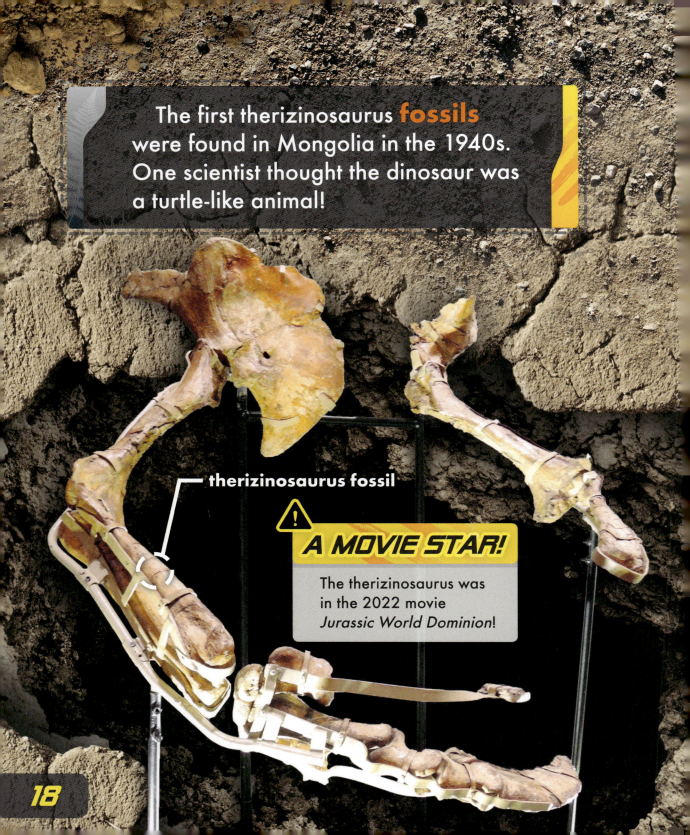

The first therizinosaurus **fossils** were found in Mongolia in the 1940s. One scientist thought the dinosaur was a turtle-like animal!

therizinosaurus fossil

⚠️ **A MOVIE STAR!**

The therizinosaurus was in the 2022 movie *Jurassic World Dominion*!

# THERIZINOSAURUS FOSSIL MAP

North America

Europe

Asia

Africa

South America

**KEY**

fossil site

More discoveries proved it was a dinosaur. Scientists continue to learn about the therizinosaurus!

# GET TO KNOW THE THERIZINOSAURUS

small head

long neck

**LOCATION**
North America
Asia

long, sharp claws

**HEIGHT** around 16 feet (5 meters) tall

**LENGTH** around 33 feet (10 meters) long

20

## ERA

around 100 million to 66 million years ago during the Late Cretaceous period

**Mesozoic era**

Triassic | Jurassic | Cretaceous

## FIRST FOSSILS FOUND

Nemegt Formation, Mongolia, in 1948

## FOOD

ferns

flowering plants

## WEIGHT

over 11,000 pounds (4,990 kilograms)

21

# GLOSSARY

**asteroid**—a small rocky object that circles the sun

**Cretaceous period**—the last period of the Mesozoic era that occurred between 145 million and 66 million years ago; the Late Cretaceous period began around 100 million years ago.

**digested**—to have turned food into something the body can use

**evolved**—changed slowly into a different form

**extinct**—no longer living

**fossils**—the remains of living things that lived long ago

**habitat**—a home or area where animals prefer to live

**Mesozoic era**—a time in history in which dinosaurs lived on Earth; the first birds, mammals, and flowering plants appeared on Earth during the Mesozoic era.

**predators**—animals that hunt other animals for food

**theropod**—a meat-eating dinosaur that had two small arms and moved on two legs

# TO LEARN MORE

### AT THE LIBRARY

Braun, Eric. *Could You Survive the Cretaceous Period?: An Interactive Prehistoric Adventure*. North Mankato, Minn.: Capstone Press, 2020.

Gardner, Jane P. *How Asteroids Shaped Earth*. Minneapolis, Minn.: Jump!, 2021.

Sabelko, Rebecca. *Velociraptor*. Minneapolis, Minn.: Bellwether Media, 2020.

### ON THE WEB

Factsurfer.com gives you a safe, fun way to find more information.

1. Go to www.factsurfer.com.

2. Enter "therizinosaurus" into the search box and click 🔍.

3. Select your book cover to see a list of related content.

# INDEX

arm, 8
asteroid, 17
beak, 13
belly, 9, 13
claws, 4, 12, 15
evolved, 11
extinct, 17
fight, 15
food, 10, 11, 12, 13
fossils, 18, 19
get to know, 20–21
habitat, 17
head, 8
hips, 9

*Jurassic World Dominion*, 18
Late Cretaceous period, 5
map, 5, 19
Mesozoic era, 5
Mongolia, 18
mouth, 12
name, 9
neck, 8
predators, 14, 15
pronunciation, 5
scientists, 11, 15, 18, 19
size, 4, 6, 7, 8, 9
tarbosaurus, 14
theropod, 10

The images in this book are reproduced through the courtesy of: James Kuether, front cover, pp. 4-5, 6-7, 8-9, 10-11, 11 (all plants), 12-13, 14-15, 16-17, 20-21; praktistock, p. 9 (tool); Yuya Tamai, p. 18.